CW00434133

LIGHT

AND

DARK

A compilation of views on current topics in the news and philosophical issues expressed in a satirical and (hopefully) amusing way

Content has previously been published in separate volumes This edition also contains all relevant artworks but in black and white to minimise the purchase price

ARTUSOV

'In my beginning is my end, in my end is my beginning'

DEDICATED TO JOHN COOPER CLARKE

(if that's OK with him)

DEDICATED TO THE MEMORY OF GEORGE ORWELL

' Presenting this cornucopia

Welcome to dystopia

Goodbye to a Utopia

It's the new myopia

Everything is ropier

New leaders even dopier

Thoughts are de rigueur wokier

The news is getting soapier

Celebs becoming gropier

The descent to Hell is slopier '

LIGHT CONTENTS

3

DARK CONTENTS

Introduction

A selection of verse from the author of 'Time, Space, Taste', 'The Unquiet Gravy', 'Ah!' and 'Ha!'

A wry, cynical, satirical, tongue in cheek collection of short verses examining the current zeitgeist and influenced by George Orwell.

About the author

Seriously, does anyone want to know? - I thought not

All is agreed

The elephant in the room is greed

Too much of what you just don't need

Like all 'essentials' you dearly really want to try

We are here to live and buy

Before pushing a trolley in the great store in the sky

Buy, buy, buy, buy a tie, buy a pie, buy a lie

Bye, bye money and kiss your diet plans goodbye

You desire that facial cream to make your wrinkles a bad dream

Desired by all, Adonis, Apollo & that little man from East Cheam

What about a new kitchen and a costly watch that adds five grand

To tell the time in Gibraltar at fifty metres underwater?

A dash of perfume, smell like a trollop's bedroom

A splash of Brut to make you cute

So women will admire you in your birthday suit

Goods are good is understood, so that's sad and bad

Compulsory purchase is the order of the day

We all know who is to blame, those hidden persuaders

They are the immortal invaders to the living room

The slime spewing out from your TV set

Money circulates like blood

So you must expect to get some clots

Possession to obliterate depression

Fashion is the media's passion, the only answer is dystopia

No shops at all, and only one pair of pants

Issued when you are 18, so keep them clean

Everyone in boiler suits and hobnail boots

No cars no more, just like Orwell's 1984

A Brave New World and an awful bore

What we want is more, more, more.

As I woked out one morning

To take the air along my lane

I saw the loveliest maiden

She walked as if enchained

I knew that I could free her

For was I not a God?

Chosen words from me and she'd be free

But then I sensed the Jabber Woke, my son

It sealed my lips forever

I could not speak

I could not talk

I dare not look

If anything took place

Although I was a God

She might yell out 'You dirty little sod!'

And call PC Plod as well

So I ran off like hell

And had at pint or two at the Bell

If truth to tell

Attack of the Giant Welsh Black Lesbian Disabled Killer Vampire Slugs (Starring J. Drip and Di Rea Orifis , Cert XX)

It's got diversity

It's got perversity

It's got absurdity

It's got controversiality

And it's got SLUGS

What more do you want?

Your money back?

Award ceremonies

It seems that these are now weekly events

Awards for anything at all, e.g. 'Best Supporting Wall'

Any excuse for Luvvie excess

New outfits: God! A ghastly dress & who looks the biggest mess?

Who's had their face lifted again? Never mind their pelvic floor

Botox, small cocks and the big knobs co-exist

Teeth are a-gleaming and glowing fluorescent white

Now let's have those speeches, plenty of screeches & whooping

Sincerity is faked, make-up is caked, red carpet for the day

You've got what it fakes, you live in LA

Or Beverley Hills, a pointless place of no thrills

'I'd like to thank everyone', gush from the mush

Becomes the norm except where there's a hint of porn

Then it's 'I'd like to SPANK everybody ....'

The limos are gathering, the Press is still slavering

It's over and done, but another one soon

Ceremonies, ephemeral memories, cocaine spoons under LA moon

The birds

A nightingale busked in Berkeley Square

A starling flew in Barking

A crow went slow in scenic Hounslow

A sparrow went to seed near Bow Bells

A pigeon muting in Tooting

Birds of a feather got together near Big Ben

But they couldn't compete with Great Tit in No. 10

The BJ blues (to the tune of All Along The Watchtower)

There must be some kind of money here

Said the PM to his thief

There's too much confusion, it's caused by all my briefs

Business men, they buy me wine

Make jokes about my girth

None are on the level, that's fine

And I never keep my word

No reason to get exited (sic)

My chief he kind of spoke

There are many here among us, who feel you're but a joke

You and I, we know you're just a twat

And this, our undeserved fate

So let's continue talk for now

The booze is getting late

All along with this shower

'priceless!' was the view

While all the admin came and went, bare faced robbery too

Outside in the resistance, a wild public began to howl

"The creatures.... looked from pig to man, and from man to pig.... but it was impossible to say which was which." ('Animal Farm': George Orwell)

18

Blonde moments

Check today's agenda

Then confirm your name tag gender

Maybe go on a bender

After work? Reprise your great pretender?

You lie helplessly in fate's blender

You lie hopelessly to the wife

You lie throughout your privileged life

You dress to the right but lean to the left

Your life is surveyed and mapped out

A road of excess, around the bend

Roundabouts that never end

Bounders and louts are your best friends

Rounds of drinks that always extend

Drinking to the bitter end

It's destiny and density

Futility in colossal immensity

Density starts from the top

Underneath the blonde baboon's unruly mop

Of hair today and gone tomorrow

Your parting is a thing of sorrow

Where have all the showers gone?

Gone to Gotham City and Gomorrah everyone

Long time grasping

Gone to Queer Street, gone to Bedlam

Gone to Funny Farm, gone to the casket

The past that will always malinger

The present like a flickering flame

A fleeting dance of empty fame

River of denial for the blame

Futures swirling in witches' cauldrons

Containing drab's newborn tiny finger

Something useless this way comes

Achievement needs more than just stuck up thumbs

A deep knock from the very depths of hell

Sounding like a distant knell

The Grand Inquisitor, he sees all

The Grand Inquisitor will come to make a call

He will torture this from you

'Just exactly what did you ever do?'

(Apart from bluster, lie and party too)

20

The Canterbury fails

He looks like a banker, and a bit of a ranker

Never mentions God, to avoid any rancour

• His apparel comes straight from bad taste hell

Good Lord! It really is an unholy joke

A psychedelic shower curtain is his cloak

A pointy tea cosy for his bonce

Does this really help the congregation's response?

What's the point of looking a complete ponce?

A white frilly shirt, a front clip board sealed with 4 lumps of choc

All topped with a large bent stick and looking a bit crook

Long time, no Holy See through all this garish finery

Isn't it time he returned to the word of God

And stopped bashing the bishop

The dirty old sod

Crummy afternoon

The power company has taken all my dosh

And left me with a fiscal loss

On a sunny climate change afternoon

I sit here with ice cream and spoon

And I can't even float my boat

From now on none will get my vote

This mug of tea tastes like creosote

All I've got is my astro turf

And some slightly flaky scurf

The wife's gone off to nasty, perspiring Dubai

With no goodbye and 'Get it here' tattoo on upper thigh

Totty's nicked my new bike, off with a woman – what a dyke!

I'm OK – what's not to like? Signed up with a dating agency

Let's see what women are now free, will they get the hots for me?

My God! Look at that! And I paid a mighty fee

I suppose buggers can't be choosers

There's always boozers for the losers

Or one of those ghastly geriatric cruises

TOILETS

24

Dalek conquest 3023 AD

His Royal Dalek Bit-Ram-III-Tetra-Flips

Asked fellow Daleks around for bits and chips

The last human had finally expired, helped by friendly high voltage wire

No more nasty body waste

No more need for wallpaper paste

No more vulgarity or bad taste

Mrs Tracy Dalek served up celebration electrons

Jolly good show, what-ho, chaps, Bit-Ram said

Extermination's worth getting out of bed

Let's watch some ancient history

On something they once called TV

It's a weekly comedy, PMQs to me and thee

Followed by a nice surprise, I've found an unknown

Morecombe and Wise, it's worth a butcher's

Then I'll read my poetry followed by the hits of Showaddywaddy

The self-assembled did not hesitate

'SELF-EXTERMINATE!'

'SELF-EXTERMINATE!'

Darts

Tired of life?

Failed to make life's charts?

Not too bothered about the marital arts?

Do you have beer delivered in large carts?

Are you lacking functioning parts?

And always enjoy setting light your farts?

Isn't it time you took up Darts?

Deny everything

Are you Boris Johnson? **No**

But you were once the Prime Minister? **No, I wasn't**

Oh, come on, Mr Johnson - It's me - Harriet Harman **No, it isn't**

But you are not the hard-working and diligent MP for Uxbridge?

 No I'm not

Did you understand the simple rules you wrote yourself? **No**

Mr Johnson, this is a House of Commons Privileges Committee Enquiry **No, it isn't**

Mr Johnson - Do you ever answer a question honestly? **No**

Thank you, you may step down, kiss the lawyers we paid for and claim expenses again

Please take all the urine you have extracted with you

Derriere care

My botty must always have the best

A Botti-celli-ish bum-fest

A cosy tincture for my sphincter

Only the softest purest sheets will do

To manage that unspeakable to-do

Whiter than white is essential

Tested by those fluffy puppies

De-rigueur for aspiring yuppies

Double cushioned

'..Provide Ultimate Quilted Comfort with Unique Air Pocket..'

Mmmmm....gotta, gotta, gotta, get, get, get

Now your crevice will not sue for neglect

A paper Rex that protects your kecks

Banish skid marks

Banish chance of potential shame

If perchance an accident became

Nurses in the A and E might see

Big jobs demand soft answers

So treat yourself

Spoil your arse

Show some class

Your are not a snob

So save the Daily Mail for another big job

Save the Sun and don't be a knob

Donate them to your local yob

So be kind to your behind, and restore the nation's glory

Think grateful cheeks

Then think Ordure! Ordure!

Then think Tory

(excrement in all its glory)

Digital money just ain't funny

Digital money is on its way

Cash as passé as Fay Wray

Going shopping? Better think twice

Buying too much is not very nice

You bought a jumper just last year

We think it was a smidgen just too dear

One for now must simply suffice

That's the second today! I mean another pizza!

No, no, no, say the Obesity Polizza

Tyburn once was for public hanging

Now we'll revive it for public weighing

We can manage things for you

We can now ensure what you should do

We will even test your daily poo

All because we really love you

We can notice what you read

We record your every deed

We will monitor your daily feed

Freedom isn't what you really want

29

Too much makes you incontinont (sic)

We can recompense for past slavery and injustice

Your racial memory might show you were a Roman slave

Are you Celtic? We'll make those Anglo-Saxon bastards pay!

What did the Romans ever do for us?

It might seem funny to do without real money

No pounds and pence

But it does make sense

Our aim is to make life easier for you

Now we control your stash

A whip-round of the monetary lash

We can arrange your happy hour

We can supply your happy gas

Your money can't buy you happiness

So we've taken it all away, oh yes!

It's all because we really love you

Do we have your best interests at heart?

Truth to tell, we couldn't really give a fart

It's dog meet dog

Yes, Crufts, woof, woof, ruff, ruff, ruff

Unleash the dogs of the floor

For Fido and Rover to strut, strut, strut

It's the dogs' bollocks and bitches to do their stuff

The audience are reporters all, they all have a scoop

For the inevitable poop, poop, poop

Beware the savage jaw, and that's just the owner, for sure

Please don't think I am somewhat barking

I love dogs, they are mostly for the good

(e.g. a dog would never invent Hollywood)

Unconditional love is what they give

Total loyalty, better than some I could mention

Dog days, dog tired, dog in a manger, a spot of dogging

If only the nation DID go to the dogs

To give us all a true doggy style loyalty

I say the average dog is smarter than its master

So this is what really hurts me in my head

Why do the breeds have to be SO in-bred?

Economical with the truth

Is the Treasury really a national treasure?

And does it give us any pleasure?

Gilts, gilts, gilts, they have a Gilt Complex, I bet

Inflation gives us consternation

Blow up dolls and miscegenation

Stagflation gives us constipation

Fiscal drag, I need a fag , GDP, what's in it for me?

Gloom and doom and then perhaps a boom

Give me some credit, I know about debt, and is there still money
for free?

Ponzi means Pyramid schemes, not for Mummies but for dummies

The ERM, what was it? Just 3 letters

Don't ask questions of your betters

Paper money, men of straw

Plastic cards, indices and more

The City of London, is she a whore?

I'm not bothered, my money's under my mattress

And my maitresse is lying on top, so time for pussy pop

Euro-derision song contest

Beyond belief, beyond hope

Beyond the pale, beyond the bucket

Beyond the dark, beyond comprehension

Beyond the yonder, beyond wonder

Beyond explanation, beyond expletives

I have to admit I am totally defeated

Unfortunately for me......IT'S BEYOND PARODY

PS What next: The Eurovision Thong Contest?

Evil breakfast

By the sticking of my crumbs

Wicked breakfast in bed is simply dumb

(thank you so much, Mr Macbeth – Didn't those witches have such bad breath!)

•

Fear and loathing in Woking

Evening classes still available

Bring a copy of the Daily Malentable

Free to all those quite incapable

Filthy shades of grey

All those ways to enjoy? No way!

Know ye, sodomy is not for me

Abstention is the way to be

I'd rather have a cup of tea

Than indulge in position missionary

Congress always frightens all the horses

Nice ladies never go down on golf courses

Not now! Save it fellater!

Even educated fleas do it, Noel Coward once remarked

But he meant they fell in love, and I love someone very dearly

That person, well it's very clearly, it's me, naturally

Loving one cannot misfire, I even love my middle tyre

What is there not to admire? Full of sincere lust and desire

Jezebel was part of the Devil's plan

And she could bake a mean quiche flan

It all began when Eve ate the fruit

Became conscious of her birthday suit

Adam found her rather cute

He liked the way she blew his flute

Glastonbury torture

An annual pilgrimage, with the emphasis on grim

To Funny Farm for lots of slush n' slurry

There's plenty of it, no need to hurry

Enjoy a boggy field with uninviting commodes

Queues for ever for Portaloos, poo, poo, poo

The food's a bit suspicious too

But you are here for aural assault

It's music to your ears, not for your old dears

It's all intense if that makes sense

For lustful youth it's just the ticket

You can do it in a thicket

But at what price? The cost of such discomfort

Is three hundred 60 smackers so you must be crackers

I saw the Who, this is true, in '65 for 20 pence....Now that DID make sense

God - I hate shopping

God said 'Tough luck, son, it's got to be done'

Don't forget my beer and my 20 Benson

I called on disciple Peter and we took electric bikes

The Xmas muzak was blaring and very, very wearing

'Do they know it's Xmas?': NO, It was actually October

'I wish it could be Xmas every day': NO WAY

I was informed I was walking in a Winter Wonder Land

In Tesco, Dagenham? This was difficult to understand

I'd never seen so much cream and cheese

And that creamed 'Whisky' - yuck - yuck - yuck

Only a schmuck would drink that muck

Nat King Cole or Bing went 'Ting a ling a ling'

All that crap really does my head in

They sang 'A rup pa pa pum'

That really got right up my bum

Noddy Holder screamed over my shoulder

Real Xmas was so totally belied

It was all so much worse than being crucified

Hello darkness in my glass

I've come to drink with you again

I'm here to sup you up, that's plain

Other flavours cannot you surpass, chilled Guinness is just bliss

'I drink therefore I am'..........a dedicated Guinness fan

A daily dose I cannot bear to miss

Better than any fizz, 'Tis really is the bizz

It simply, simply is just 'IS'

A strange brew that's good for you, I do enjoy a pint or two

So creamy, so dreamy, up to the mark

My taste buds do like being in the dark

Hippy homage

A long time ago I was a Hippy

My kaftan was cool, my candles were drippy

The waiter delivered my free range bean curd

Wow, that's too much, man, so he whipped half away

I said that ain't cool, cat, don't be a turd

The other dudes with me all fell about

I think they'd all had too much Mary-Jane clout

The vegan joint was not 'Bogarted' by the way

Things became outa-sight but how can you tell?

I tuned in, turned on and hit the sack

In those days minds were blown, but blow jobs were almost unknown

I got into ZEN, 'Less is more' (well, more or less)

But my Old Lady said 'Heavy' - So she put me on a diet

I said 'Far Out', she said yes, 'Far out of the bedroom, please

It's where it's at and please stop wearing that ridiculous hat'

I had to agree I did look a twat, the times they were a-changing

I was skint and wasn't earning any bread

So I became a Hedge Fund manager instead

The hologram men

Shifting, slinking, sleazy shapes

The lights are on but all are out

Brightness (in a luminescence sense), lightness to deceive

Gravity is nowhere present to perceive

Talking, porking, and some norking

Life goes slightly on, the limp are walking

Ministers make their vows

All are futures, never nows

The House is ignorant of the nous

Bread and circuses

Burger and Strictly

KFC and Mrs Brown's boys

Pot noodle is right up the Street

Make sure life is just a game

Even if you lose at home again

Forgotten heroes underground

Rest peacefully from madness up above

Hologram men so hollow

There's only so much we all can swallow

Holy emergency contacts

You may find praying to these Saints useful for particular problems

Saint Arnold of Soissons (Beer)

Saint Matthias The Apostle (Alcoholics)

Saint Dymphna (Mental Disorders)

Saint Bonadventure (Bowel Disorders)

Saint Rita of Cascia (Impossible Causes)

Saint Drogo (Coffeehouses)

Saint Antony of Padua (Lost Items)

Saint Julian the Hospitaller (Murderers)

Saint Genesius of Arles (Chilblains and Scurf)

Saint Lidwina (Ice Skaters)

Saint Giles (Breast Feeding and Lepers)

Saint Fiacre (Victims of venereal disease, haemorrhoids and fistulas, taxi cab drivers, box makers, florists, hosiers)

I cast the runes

Ate some prunes

Read my stools

Did the I-CHING

Eschewed the FENG-SHUI

Re-oriented my bed

My privates now face the right way instead

Dealt a mean TAROT- picked the best of three

Consulted all the horoscopes

Mercury was ascendant in Uranus

Something was on the cusp

Venus came between us

Mars bars got in the Milky Way

Met Mrs Palm and her five daughters whilst reading my lines

Looked at my tea leaves after cutting the bag

Gazed at the crystal ball

The difference it made was just bugger all

Que sera, sera, whatever will be, will be

So don't bother me with all that cosmic debris

I don't want to go to heaven

I have been so very good

Always did just what I should, always finished all my pud

Gave five pence to charity when I could

When a wolf in the dark and wild, wild wood

Never molested Little Red Riding Hood

Adjusted trousers if got wood

Constantly cared for neighbourhood

I have banished naughty thoughts obtuse

Baden Powell warned me against 'self-abuse'

Never had a wet dream or needed vaseline

Never needed to be obscene

When I depart the human race

No need to enter the state of grace

Straight to heaven I regret

I do not relish all that praising

Lunch with Cliff and Mary, hardly spirit raising

So I will just protest and refuse to enter

And remain in the reception centre

I enjoy nothing

Nought is my port of thought, nothing is eternal

Nothing can't be got rid of, noughty is my forte

You cannot filch zilch, avoid a void for it can be nothing

(The empty voids are worst)

It's the hole in the chicken without the stuffing

Now those Romans didn't really bother with nothing

Arabs invented 'nothing', figs and figures, meat and drink to them

Roman times were tricky without nothing

Multiply MCMDLXIV by XIX, and crap your kecks

I met a centurion, he was a Mancunian

He had a chariot, his wife was called Harriet

I said 'amicus, do this multiplication'

He started to do a lot of huffing n' puffing

He finally said 'Oh XXXX XX!'

Which of course was wrong, so it proved my point, BONG!

You can't get away without nothing

We had a good laugh, jumped into his chariot

Stopped off at the Chariot and Horses

For 16 pints and 3 main courses

I stand to be corrected

As Ms Whiplash directed

But Political Correction?

It's hard to comply and I can see why

The 'N' word is now taboo, or the outlook will be black for you

(I don't suppose you can say that too)

For us lovers of Rap, we say that's just crap

For Rappers non Caucasian use the 'N' word on many an occasion

And pity poor old 'N', that faithful hound of a VC Hero

His grave was desecrated and his name reduced to zero

So spare us all that Wokey-Wokey palaver

It just gets me into a frightful lather

I want to be a rock n' roll star

Sing the Blues, bend that note, change name to Doctor Deep Throat

Enjoy the fame, earn a groat and float my boat

Buy a castle with a moat, see how long a Rolls Royce stays afloat

Get a trophy wife, soak in the booze, the best of all is mine to choose

Know seventh heavens suspended, augmented and diminished

Be sharp or success could fall flat

Major, Minor, Pentatonic and gin and tonics

Adoring fans, autographs and naughty frolics

Get that adrenalin rush on stage

Cause the usual tour hotel outrage

And avoiding a Janis, Jim or Jimi 'experience' would be sage

I went down to the cross roads

Got down on my knees

I asked the Lord above for mercy

And a tenner for a feed

But he was on the golf course, did not hear my need

Went back down to the cross roads

It was now near midnight

I offered my soul to Satan

For a Walnut Whip Delight

The Devil was into detail, he'd spent his life in retail

Showed me the Contract - said sign it in blood

ALL eternity? Get lost - you greedy little sod

He buggered off in his Reliant Robin

With his chauffeur Oddjob to go shoppin'

And I was left with zilch

Desperately I rang up Zeus, his phone was off the hook

I then called Odin in Valhalla

But he'd got slayed on mead

So it had to be the Food Bank for a feed

I really was in desperate need

Incubus and succubus

These are demons (male and female) that might molest you at night

When Morpheus imposes

They encourage their victims to be rather risque

I'm game, so that's OK

But you'd think they would phone first so you can take some Listerine

Before it gets a bit too obscene

The problem is you can wait forever for a lush succubus

Then three come along all at once

Just popping off to see 20 million years AD

Bought a spaceship, Amazon (post free)

Guaranteed to forever supply '1 g'

(That's Earth gravitational acceleration to you and me)

Loaded up Artificial Reality

Plus a brewery, naturally

Plus a steak and chips simulator

Plus a distillery creator

Plus Randy Rachel (deluxe version)

Catering for all perversion

Accelerating at 1 g, I will reach near the speed of light

In about one year if I am right

When within one million millionth of that pace

The time dilation Einstein says that I will face

Will be about a million times, so the 20 years - my time in space

Will be 20 million years that you on Earth will face

[Ships Log: 20 years hence]

Returned to Earth and launched a drone

Oh dear, it seems I am alone

The only life is giant cockroaches

They had evolved both lungs and heart

So now were bigger than a dustman's cart

(A nuclear war had played its part)

So I'm now off to the Forbidden Planet

To meet Altaira for a beer

(Of course none of you will get this last text – but what the heck)

Kung phew

I was once a low down cheap little punk

There was nothing but nothing I would not flunk

Mum said 'It's about time you showed some spunk

So I've booked you in to become a Shaolin Warrior monk'

'You'll learn all about **Yi Jin Jing**

Which cannot be such a bad thing'

Oh! I thought, such a misfortune cookie

Oh! I contemplated - no more nookie

So off to China for **Yin and Yang**

Every day I was trained to endure a lot of pain

My nuts were kicked without refrain

Every day for six hundred days

Buddha works in mysterious ways

I banged my head against the wall

For ten hours daily and just a bowl of rice

Change the body, change the mind

Change the mind, change the body

Qi is the key

Then a bit of **Shen**

Shen works through with the **Yi**

(Yes, there is still brown rice for tea)

Yi works out within the **Qi**

Qi works with body, can't you see?

After that comes **Ting**

Followed by **Song Kua**

Then develop your **Dan Tians**

Leading to **Shi San Tai Bao**

This translates as the '**Thirteen Wonders'**

This describes the **Eight Gates** and the **Five Elements**

Finally one gets to discharge your power

Now the mind controls the body

Concentrated energy through the palm

Break those bricks

Get your kicks

On Kung Phew Route 66

Hang huge rocks from your testicles

Whilst climbing up five flights of stairs

Banishing all life's tribulations and existential blips

All that's missing is steak and chips

The last hedgehog

His name was Colin and he lived near Andover

Didn't get run over, know it was over, didn't know he was the last

And nor did anyone else, caring was past

Except 500 fleas who are now in mourning

Leave your body

I did not leave my heart in San Francisco

I considered leaving it to carrion, 'al fiasco'

But then got an offer from pet food firm in Hounslow

I left my ego and my spleen

To a dank corner of East Cheam

I left a leg to a Mystic Smeg

Giving the forecasts something worth a dreg

I left my wit to the city of Phuket

I left my naughty little ding-a-ling

To the exotic town of tiny Tring

I left my airs to brassy Broadstairs

I left my body odour smells

To the Bishop of Bath and Wells

I left my knees to Stockton on Tees

I donated my bot to debonair Didcot

I left the rest to my local food bank

Though by now a trifle rank

Recycle your body, donate your cadaver

It could enhance a needy person's larder

Life was fun (remember?)

Remember when you were young?

And lots of people drank 'Blue Nun'?

And the news was seldom spun

Page 3 gave young men some fun

Thinking was left up to one

100 was then a ton

Agreements meant things were done

As holy as a naked nun

Not merely 'Oven Ready' fun

Sergeant majors screamed out '...'SHUN!'

In Blackpool always shone the Sun

Tasty was a Hot Cross bun

One could crack a black and white pun

Did you jump the starting gun?

Now life's a circular unforgiving run

Lottery winner

Mr John Hugh Willoughby

Won 10 million on the Euro Lottery

Unfortunately, he was now a creaky 83

But undeterred he glugged two full schooners of tonic wine

Asked the wife what would she like, she thought a while and said

A new bell for her trusty, rusty old bike

A world cruise, a Rolls Royce, maybe?

Big decisions need a nice strong pot of tea

It's remarkable the friends they never knew they had

Including relatives who lived in Chad

A mansion in St John's Wood looked nice

But we've lived in Neasden all our life

A chauffeur and a Roller by jingo

But just to drive to local Bingo?

The trouble with those world cruise ships

You can never get real fish and chips

They both indulged – yes, silken thermal underwear!

They bought the Big Issue for the very first time

An extra gin and tonic is no crime

Nor is tequila with a twist of lime

The family had been long estranged

But odd to say, they all turned up again

A Rolex for me, a Rolex for you?

A diamond collar for the poodle?

A bigger cuttlebone for the budgie?

A bigger screen to watch a bigger 'Strictly'?

Decisions, decisions are killing me

Look, let's discuss this over tea

Luvvie dovey

Tread the boards

Perform in pantomime

'Darling, darling, you were simply just divine!'

(even in Newcastle under Lyme)

Only enter left of stage

Exit to the right and affect self-righteous rage

It's difficult to avoid the right wing hordes

'Darling, I am simply so abhorred

I never got my so deserved award!'

'I know darling – it's just simply ghastly!

This salsa verde has so little parsley!'

Progressive acting improves one vastly

Oscars for everyone, even the extras

Lots of kissing, lots of mmm-waahs and a royal curtsy

Don't tell them you still live with Mum in Chertsey

Never mind your tiny part, this could be the starry start

Starlets, harlots plus lines so far from good

That you might end up in Hollywood

(which makes a change from Harold Wood, Essex)

A stint on the deeply unlovable South Bank

You have the Arts Council to thank

Squeeze into those Shakespearean tights

Transportation to the Globe's delights

Lead on, Macduff, but never say

The actual name of the Scottish play

Boycott and girlcott Snow White and the Seven Dwarfs

Unless it's Neutral Tint & Seven Metrically Challenged Persons

Carry on acting, a season in Clacton but where's the action?

Peers upon piers, cheers from old dears, claps from the chaps

Tread and pray the boards don't end up in the Norfolk Broads

Actresses are now called actor – well, both revel in Max Factor

If you die on stage, make it up, the peasants will just lap it up

It's bums on seats and you don't need a quote from Keats

Treats, no empty seats, embracing greets, drinkies and meets

Live for the applause, that adrenaline rush, a royal flush

Autograph seeking hordes of wannabe fans

'Oh darling! Such dirty, grubby sweaty hands!'

Final curtain, gone for a Burton

Take your bow, take your fee, thank God for Actors' Equity

Lying rap

Lies, lies, and lies, more than the flies on acres of putrefying meat pies

No surprise, hence so few 'Whys? Like a million pixels before our eyes

People gasp their pointless sighs, influencers just flaunt their thighs, MPs kiss integrity good bye and deny, futures die, so people, please do get wise

It's your demise, so don't go to beddy-byes and close your eyes

It's time to arise, claim your prize, claim the skies, claim the land

Take your future in your hand or just go out and just get canned

Parvenu rap

I'm a parvenu, my woman's a marvenu

You bet your ass, I'm a marvel too, made it through

So well to do, too bad about you, oh boo-hoo-hoo

Got a Chelsea pad, got a castle loo, got a seaside view

Move in the right circles, keep in shape, make them gape

Loud and never square, always there, never turn a hair

Wherever I look celebs are there - 'hello, how do you screw?

Back of the Roller do for you?'

Next venue, more chit chat, know it off pat

Style guru, one of the few, influencer too

Yeh, I'm a frivolous lascivious invidious son of a bitch

White powder up my snitch, I've got principles to ditch

'Hi, babe! Hollywood fit? Let's see you without a stitch'

My ghost writer's arrived, essential for a spiced up bio

Telling porkies about my early struggles and the strife so

Let's add extra spouse, a life in Scouse in a one-bed house?

It will be a top seller giving me yet another big cellar

To lay down that Lafite, so indiscrete, and the tax man cheat

And it's always Lobb footwear on my feet..... 'ain't I a treat?'

Position zugzwang

So let it hang, zip up the wang

Delay big bang, stall the tang

Endure the pang, avoid the wicked witches' fang

Be a gently idling purring pink Mustang

Aim for Ying and Yang, so join a finely balanced gang

Broker rang and advised to let position hang

Chauffeur rang and said he'd had a prang

Yes, it was Mr Zhang Chang speaking Cockney rhyming slang

The Bentley's ding-dang came with a resounding clang

This then that, tit for tat, makes everything so very thrang

Elsewhere, in a nick, the surly suspect sang

Faced by a finger-printed heroin meringue

And a nicked vase from the dynasty of Shang

His lawyer told him his sentence could be strang

The villain said 'You can cut my porridge, you're so trang'

In Coventry a wannabe Keith Richards went ker-twang

And climaxed with a kwrang-a-lang-a-dang-a-lang

Like a cacophonous sarcophagus Gotterdammerang

Worse than the hollering of an Old Etoniang Orangutang

Punk groups that never quite made it

Colostomy Explosion

The Flying Faeces Brothers

The Cottaging Pies

Wayne and the Anchors

The Abortive Chandeliers

Abhorrent Vacuum Cleaners

Onanist

The Petulant Panties

Satanic Mechanics

Blond Baboon and the Cabinet

Shakin' Simon and the Shirt Tail Lifters

The Sodomy Sisters

Lobotomy

The Spitting Zit-Gits

Thrusting Tadpoles

Syphilitic Sandbags

Boris and the Body Fluids

The Bashful Bellends (Formerly 'The Swinging Bellends')

Cross-Dresser, Pills, Trash and Dung

Radio caca

Radio 1: It's no fun

Radio 2: Rather sniff glue, have a poo or spew

Radio 3: Too dreary for me

Radio 4: What a bore

Radio 5: Oh, I say why oh why?

Listen, this is most profound - something I've always found:

These radio stations are great BUT WITHOUT THE SOUND

Reds under the bed

Why under the bed?

When they could be in your bed?

If she's nice and Slavic

And discusses the dialectic

With something electric

Rather eclectic

Possibly asymmetric, with good vibrations

She might grab your curlies

Talking heads, giving head

Jaw-jaw is better than war-war

But you can't beat a good woman

Unless she's into S & M

And respects British phlegm

And says come again

A stiff upper lip, a witty quip

A Freudian slip

A dry martini, shaken not stirred

For James Bond and his bird

War is absurd

East meets west: which position is best?

There's a lot of dis-Putin'

There could be some shootin'

I like detente

In flagrante my penchant

I favour deterrent

So embrace all your Reds, however repellent

Back in the Kremlin, those commies are a-trembling

The Foreign Office sends a warning

The Kremlin cats must all be yawning

A new era should be dawning

As when Gorbachev meet Maggie T.

That's quite enough from me

Sayings of wisdom revisited

'The journey of a thousand miles begins with ....**lots of waiting, queues, smelly toilets and over-priced refreshments**'

'That which does not kill us makes us ......**lucky**'

When the going gets tough, the tough...... **either beat you up or hire a lawyer**'

'You only live once ..... **which saves the cost of another funeral**'

'Tis better to have loved and lost than ..... **got married**'

'If you are going through hell, ... **turn off the M25 at the nearest junction**'

'There's a time and place for everything'..... EXCEPT:

The song 'Kumbaya, My Lord', whistling, postcards of views of Swindon, and chewing gum

'Tomorrow is another **pizza leaflet**'

'Tomorrow and tomorrow and tomorrow **- three pizza leaflets**'

The secret tryst of Putin's aroma therapist:

Vlad enjoys a scent, but hates dissent

He loves a whiff and taut midriff

Wakes in the morning but won't smell the coffee

Until it's been tasted for poison, then a quick cup

With a Novichokky bar, the one that 'Helps you dictate, arrest and slay'

It's a smell of power after a power shower in a Kremlin tower

Then it's a dab of oil here, a dab of oil there

He thinks he's a swell with all of that smell

He thinks this deters the West who is doing its best

To sap his 'Precious Bodily Fluids' through his vest

Vlad says 'It's a conspiracy by the druids, and giant arachnids'

Some say Vlad is tad mad and a bad sad cad to boot

To others he's just a bit of laddy

Who jokes with his caddy and swings his club

And just enjoys a soak in his tub

And a drink of two in his local private heavily guarded secret pub

The sewage monster

It ate Westbury

It thought it was just slurry

Give ye thanks for a true miracle

Nothing here to see, move on, no worry

Timmy works at CCHQ

If working is the word

He's in by eleven on Tuesday, the lazy little nerd

He got the post when mummy made a request

And promised a bequest

He's helped out by Leticia, Jocasta and Sebastian

The ladies are always out shopping and Seb just comes out

Luncheon at the Ritz, Annabel's or The Ivy is the order of the day

Timmy is in charge of the traditional tea: best bone china with dainty cakes from Fortnum and Mason

Every day, at one o'clock, right on the dot, a Bentley purrs outside

It's mummy with Timmy's lunch, smoked salmon and cucumber sandwiches and half a bottle of Mumm champers

Lady Virginia likes to ride out

And trample hunt saboteurs

On Treacle Foot, her fine old nag

Timmy has to check the conveniences are spotless

That Little Gove has done his big job

A Roller arrives, it's good old uncle Bertie

He plays the harmonium and stores Vlad's polonium

Oligarchs are happy as mudlarks to bung a few to CCHQ

Turned out nice again in SE21

A pleasant stroll in Dulwich park

With Anthrax no doubt plotting dirty deed

With Jocasta and Leticia struggling manfully on

Yes, life is pretty good it seems to me

Civilisation is all that I can see

Grass, water, wind, duck and flower

Impervious to the Tory shower

Life's energy flows around and throughout old London town

Anthrax scooped, super-doop, Barbour is snug, feeling smug

Time costs money so check by Patek

Giving you a most exclusive time

Time for home, the rain is now tipping

Time for Sunday lunch with organic dripping

Time for Bordeaux – a dose of red terroir

That will show them....Ha Ha Ha!

Mentally plan meetings for next week

Diversity, inclusivity, fraternity but no chance of drinkable tea

Bordeaux snooze, listen to news

Listen, Sunak: 'Je t'accuse!'

Whatever happened to these famous lovers?

Odysseus and Penelope: Ensconced in bungalow by the sea

Lancelot and Guinevere: Run a fitness spa that's very dear

Macbeth and Lady Macbeth; He is a chef and she's gone deaf

Romeo and Juliet: Own a dog grooming parlour with a lot of debt

Adam and Eve separated last Xmas Eve

Heloise and Abelard: She makes cheese and he makes lard

Napoleon and Josephine: Stand up comics and quite obscene

Antony and Cleo: He does burglary, she's a crossing lady: 'Stop and Go'

Paris and Helen became a trio on meeting Ben

Dante and Beatrice: Have a burger van in Bognor Regis

Tristan and Isolde: Swingers - you should see their photos folder!

Woke up this morning

Well, I woke up this morning

Felt awful, then realised I'd become immortal

Made coffee, toast with butter and marmalade

Just two slices suffices, I was on a diet

But the thought then occurred, don't be absurd

You can't die even if you have a third

Now that I had become a god, I rang up heaven

I could have a semester with archangel Gabriel's sister

But she had just left to go clubbing, so I missed her

So it was off to Mount Olympus for some dinner

But only ambrosia was on the bill, I'm not eating that pig swill

I looked in on Satan, he does a good snack and the plates are always hot

Ate a rare porterhouse from the slaughterhouse with chips

Swilled down with a Lafite 2005, so I smacked my lips

Heard all the small talk e.g. Hitler and Stalin were now an item

Got back to my pad and told my woman that I'd now live forever

She said 'You're drunk again and I've reached the end of my tether'

Xmas: excess trash

On the first day of 'XY-gene-equality-mas'

My partner sent to me

An image from the picket line

Showing so much solidarity

On the second day of XYmas

My other partner Amazoned to me

(the Post Office were on strike you see)

2 face masks and some other items of PPE

On the third day of XYmas, my broker emailed me

3 tax avoidance schemes followed by a mighty fee

On the fourth day of XYmas, my domestic gave to me

4 ironed bow ties and a cup of organic free range tea

On the fifth day of XYmas, the au-pair gave to me

5 flirty winks, 4 dirty looks, 3 shifty wiggles, 2 naughty giggles

One packet of three and a knee trembler in the pear tree

On the remaining days of whatever, my dominatrix gave to me

A spanking good time but the bottom line was not for free

(and if I hear this dirge again I will go potty)

Adding up correctly (politically)

Two add two used to make four but before George Orwell's 1984

Now we must decolonise mathematics

Decolonise nefarious nebulous naughty number tricks

Check your answers are correct in every political way

Equations must be about equality, I say

$E = mc^2$ said Albert Einstein

(E = Equality = mostly X clearly X confusion)

The square on the hypotenuse

Can amuse - hypots are often in the news

(caused Pythagoras to scratch his arse and enthuse)

Two minuses make a plus, but don't swallow this at all

Or it will go through your colon

And surprise, surprise, it gets colonised!

Number can make you dumber

Calculus is a lot of fuss, geometry gets you into shape

I want my final countdown to be Carol Vordermaned

Before refused entry to the Promised Land

666 is the number of the Beast, they say

(but he never answers anyway)

All chip in

The chips are down, the chips will fly

Chips off old blocks, but chips are in

You won't be chipper: you will be chipped

You will have had your (surgical) chips

So we know just where you are

So you don't go too far, and stray

Off the straight and very narrow way

Your pets are chipped, did they complain?

Chips on shoulders, no, chips in brain

It is futile to resist, your thoughts are clipped

Another bitter tot of dystopia is sipped

Life's now a big dipper with only dips

Praise your masters through puckered lips

Yes, we decided what you dreamt last night

Welcome to the machine, my friends

Welcome a nightmare that never ends

Who is really to blame, a culprit we can name?

It's you and I, the human's curse

To fly too close to the Sun then fall to Earth

Aspidistra vista 1936

The aspidistra looks forlornly down

Besides the pot, in dark crevice, a cockroach lurks

Upstairs a bed bug relaxes in its cosy world

Outside, through a yellow sooty haze

The sun sends out some hopeful rays

Along the road to Wigan Pier

A road paved with very few intentions

One way with definitely no pretensions

Save to survive the shrouded days

The careworn housewife scrubs her step

A distant steam train happily chuffs and clanks goodbye

Spinsters heave a lonely sigh

Delicious faggots cry - choose me!

At the butchers, take me home for tea!

Maybe tripe or a piece of liver

In this grey, grubby but proud land

Not far from chilly Blackpool sand

Coal mine, forge and football stand

A Capstan Full Strength held in hand

To do justice to this scene

Required the lens of a Robert Frank

Or eye and tripod of Bill Brandt

Or Beasley Street of John Cooper Clarke

Plus Orwellian sense of decay

But not a million miles away

The nation puts on a different mask

In Belgravia's velvet grasp

A Bertie Wooster adjusts the tie pin

Struts right out with button hole carnation

A member of the chosen nation

To visit one of many aunts

The Empire colours the globe with pink

Gin and tonic is the drink

Joins the members at one's club

For tally, bally, and I say 'what ho!'

Could these halcyon days endure?

What malevolence could possibly occur?

Nothing but parties, endless leisure

Know ye that nothing ever lasts forever

Like a bonfire night sparkler held in the hand

Far from the deep, deep sleep of fossilised England

Malignant forces bubble in hidden pustules

To plot and plan righteous national purity

To banish the shame and banish the obscurity

Aiming to avoid the mention

Of millions of the untermenschen

Aiming for a thousand heady years

But only reaping fifty million, million tears

Before, beginning, middle, end, and after

Before, they say there was then a 'Void'

An idea of which philosophers have toyed

And led many scholars to get a tad annoyed

(eventually producing Swindon - somewhere to avoid)

Then became a Beginning

Lots of lovely chances for surreptitious sinning

Hope and hoping on a prayer and a wing

In the Middle we got to do our thing

Work, eat, take a dump, sleep and maybe have a fling

Many merely molesting their beloved ding-a-ling

(and all around us, microwaves went 'ding!')

In the End, everything simply died

Punishment for food deep-fried, and a lifestyle over tried

And the knowledge that God could not be relied

Then there will be the Ever After

Nothing but nothing, save for canned laughter

At celestial ceremonies where all will win a Bafta

Could existence and non-existence ever be dafter?

Big mother is watching you

The clock strikes thirteen

Time to enjoy the Two Minutes Hate

Time to indulge in yet more monoglutamate

Fast Food makes you want to fast, fast

That greasy burger could be your last

Big Mother is watching you

The Lack of Thought Police are coming into view

They are just checking your gender's up to date

Two and two now make five?

I've got a calculator so let me check

No, this answer appears to be FOUR

But only worry if your number's up

You career will shine as long as you can count to nine

And if you have no heart, no balls, no spine

The Telescreen is all you need

Live vicariously

Live precariously

Live in a right old state and adopt the right attitude

Put up with platitude after platitude

Dystopia, myopia, everything gets ropier

Two Minutes Hate is far too short

For all leaders who can be bought

We love you Big Mother

Please tax us more

Let everyone come to our nearest shore

There's always room for just one more

In Oceania's mean and well (badly, sadly) over developed land

Black dog blues

Woke up a few times in the night

Much to my prostate's delight

My black cat then prodded me for food

Swung out of bed and put on shoes

Yes, I sleep in my semi-fetid togs

Just can't be arsed to 'Get 'em off!'

Another gloomy winter day

A piece of toast, a mug of instant

An instant mood of gradual decay

Got the black dog blues again

Tied to reality by heavy chain

Google up the gutter press

Why? Because it's free, I guess

Royal this, Royal that

Utter bollocks and crap tat

I demand a royalty

It's the usual murder, rape and gossip

'Talking stick insect found in Glossop'

Women with Botox lips abound

They always seem to be in Dubai

Or putting the sex into Essex or flying by

Got the black dog blues again

Darkness on life's empty train

Nothing ventured is the game

Mental breakdown is the name

A futile life of constant shame

One only has one's self to blame

Must escape the claustrophobic walls

Get the bus to favourite inn

Try the crossword, always get the clues going down

The blues are coming down the track

On the line, on the rack

People on the bus a-chatter, illness, children and trivial matter

Then a pint of ale and things seem better

Cannot get 19 across

Do I really give a toss?

I must surely win the Lottery one day

And banish the black dog far away

Black dog, black dog blues

Oh Lord, please bring me now life saving news

Comfortably dumb

Balance of power, balance of terror

Life beneath the nuclear umbrella

Mutually Assured Destruction (MAD)

Luckily not a huge distraction

So we can get on with our lives

A steady job, from nine to five

Shops are full of tempting morsels

Credit cards for all spending mortals

Got a car, take kids to school and to in-laws

Holidays - just fly away to a very crowded bay

But it's so much hotter than a Bognor day

It's so good the world provides

Boundless produce you might wear twice

Everything is just so nice, life gets ever better

The whole world arrives to your TV, vicariously

Sanitised for you and me

There is always fighting but it's always somewhere else

There is always a packet of biscuits on the shelf

I know our leaders will keep us safe from harm

I know there is no need for undue alarm

Just follow rules and the advice

Living in a cocooned life

Never think that this could end

Never realising that history repeats

Perhaps one day there may be no more treats

Covid

Like a bat out of Hell

Or a toucan from Wuhan

As welcome as Lord Lucan

Covid was here, causing hysterical fear

My God, we might all die!

(If only, I heard some people sigh)

The media all went ape

Gave us all graphs to gape

Oxymoronically, Whitty sang his ditty

Told us all the nitty-gritty

So it was rather a pity when forecasts were shitty

Namely: ALWAYS WRONG...........MEGA-CITY!

His forecasts made some downcast

Our Rs were incredible, never metaphorically edible

We got LOCK DOWN which didn't do a lot of good

Jobsworth Covid Marshalls were annoying arseholes

And Covid clowns decided to buy 100 bog rolls

I studied all the data and I always stayed calmer

I put on my trusty rusty suit of armour

I used my sword and pitchfork to get things from the shelves

When I got home with correct social distance

I leapt into a hot bath of Dettol at mother's insistence

My flesh began to flake off but at least I was safe

So began PPE, People Profiting Extremely

An arm and a leg just to cover one's face

And begat Test, Track and Trace and isolation

Which of course barely worked, to our consternation

And was hardly better than self-flagellation

We got a vaccine before Macron and Merkel which gave us a smirkle

Coincidentally COVID faded away before Xmas Day

The 2 million forecast cases simply caused some red faces

So it was all over and the nation was skint

Furlough had made some people a mint

We all enjoyed Lock Down and began to party

Just like the Tories, but two years later

Don't

Don't look back in anger

But look forward to the rage

Creeping and slithering to join you in old age

Don't look back at your old dreams

Or Eurydice returns with them to the Underworld

Don't gaze too far out over the sea

Or you may see the Black Sail unfurled

Don't fly too close to the Sun

To fall to Earth, your future now undone

Don't batter down the Doors of Perception

Leading to stairways down, to the sellers of self-deception

Don't cry for the Moon

But shed a salty tear instead

For those that Mars and Death have summoned to their feast

Their dogs of war are straining at the leash

These Gods link arms and summon up the blood

It's the time to feed the ravening Beast

That lurks within the dark, dark heart of man

As Ecclesiastes said: 'A time of war, and a time of peace'

Bloodthirsty conflict, never will it cease

Don't look for the Shangri-La of total bliss

You have the Garden of Earthly Delights for you to reap

To see, to touch, to taste, to make, to take, to weep

Don't consult Cassandra unless you are prepared to know

That perhaps your lifespan is measured to that very moment

Just, say, after a fall on your way home today

Like poor Berlioz at Patriach's Ponds

After his worthy life of intellectual toil

As Woland (Satan) said '...but Anna has already spilt the oil... '

For the want of nail a kingdom was lost

A wrong turning, engine stalled, millions lost was Europe's cost

Janus looks both back and forward to dispense

'Events, dear boy, events'

The wild flower meadow and the whispering trees

Silent, save for the gentle background breeze

Wispy clouds, all this surely cannot fail to please?

But don't look too closely near the ground

Peace is replaced by nature, red in tooth and claw

Everything eats everything else, with noisy jaw

Eat or be eaten, beat or be beaten

94

The Praying Mantis chooses to devour her lover

The emergent queen will slay her sisters

Don't delve too deep, the more one is to discover

Deeper and deeper until you meet the 'Quark'

Alas! We are all still in the cosmic dark

And the less one really understands

Yours not to reason why, but just to live and die

Enough of this advice, methinks

Life may present you with a balloon and pot of honey

Or the burst balloon and the empty pot

Like Eeyore, accept that this may be your lot

Dumb and dumber

Down, down, down, down

Down to the ground, ditch the concept of profound

Attention spans are shot away

What did you say? Sorry, it's just gone away

Please repeat if that's OK

No hero can be now a man

Even Superman is now a tran

The Odyssey, let's jazz it up

Add some S and M and a double G cup

Add real dick-ins into Dickens, give old Jane a pubic Eyre

And some spanking onto Bronte's wuthering tights

Add correction to Winnie and Alice

Tweedle dumb and Tweedle dumber

Modern adaptations, what a bummer

What now for Proust and Ulysses?

There's no time or need for these

Maybe madeleines with some cheesy striptease?

Bringing culture to its knees

Embers

At the dying of the embers

The goddess Hestia's spirit glows in the hearth

A man stares fixed, daydreams and remembers

Many winters, many Decembers

Sitting by the clinker, cinders and the ash

Together within the darkness of deep winter

Blackness comes with free spirit, joy, panache

There are always the reverses

There must be the obverses, two faces, light and dark

Love and hate, ecstasy and despair, good and evil

Heat from the Sun gives life, heat from furnace makes the body dust

Glowing coals, remembered goals, aims that vanished like a glance

A pirouette perfected from much pain, fleeting joy, gone again

Our subject raises crystal glass and looks through to reddish glow

A sip of spirit fires the tongue, it's so long since he was young

When the grate and the good are both out cold

When such comfort beats the bold, a life of very little to be told

Raise a glass to such a humble soul - nothing is a more truly and a more worthy goal

Emission zone lament

Do you want to drive along a road?

Who do you think you are? - Mr Toad?

The Know-Betters and the Emissions Police are getting heavy

The Bottom Inspectors are at the ready

Once a month an electric buggy can arrive

It's driverless so there's no tip

Just digital pay at £50 per trip

You could go by local bus in a sealed

Fart-proof suit, but the drawback? Bus presence is near 100 % alack

(Chorus) Oh, oh, Emission Zone, sweet memories of times alone

Sitting outside with ice-cream cone, reading an uncensored tome

You may contact people via the screen

As long as their thoughts are pure and clean

Your nutrition powder comes down the chute

You really, really must not pollute

(Chorus) Oh, oh, Emission Zone, sweet memories of times alone

Sitting outside with ice-cream cone, reading an uncensored tome

End without end

'Who wants to live forever?' sang Mercury of Queen

Not me, but no soul can bear to not exist

Not me, or do I?

When I am laid in earth, no-one will remember me

I have yet to write that symphony

(I'll ask the Devil, he has all the best tunes)

I have yet to write a Shakespearean Tragedy

I have not painted a new Madonna or a Mona Lisa

I have not chiselled a new 'Pieta'

Drop me in the river Styx with Charon giving kiss of life

So that I become immortal

Let me sense the Divine

Transpose my worthiest thoughts to a trusty robot

Without the lust, just concerns about potential rust

'And is there still WD-40 for tea?'

Let me find that magic spell

An incantation to avoid the chance of Hell

Or a chance to be reborn, a better person every time

Give me a customised new mind

So all new knowledge I can find, manual skills of every kind

Give me another 1000 years, a compromise

Send me a Muse for inspiration

For what end, just for my selfish delectation?

On this point I must reluctantly agree

So let me return to the secret gate in that garden wall

That leads to that garden, the past and future of us all

England my England

Once ruled an Empire where the Sun never set

Will always be unless you take away the parts both incongruous and ludicrous

The key is INEQUALITY and the CLASS SYSTEM

Take that away and England is gone

So keep the privilege and the snobbery and the Buck House parties

Lords, the Boat Race, all matter like a sticky wicket and blade on the feather

The Season, Royal Ascot, Henley Regatta and Cowes Week

Never turn the other cheek

Lords and Ladies, the whole aristocracy must always exist

The Bishops, the Church of England, a tug on the cassock

The Royal Family, the Establishment were Heaven sent

Private education to avoid chavs, riff-raff and the peasant

Only go Oxford or Cambridge, the two Universities

Keep the proles in their place, the Eton Mess and the Wall Game

All those Ladies in Waiting whom you won't be dating

Ladies of the Bed Chamber whom you won't be mating

Or the Lord Chamberlain will be to you castrating

Etiquette and Debretts for Old Boys club infiltrating

RELATIVITY
Copyright M S Escher company

Escher feature

When going up is going down

And going somewhere is only going round

Getting higher whilst also coming down

Smiling with perpetual frown

A grand illusion of metaphysical confusion

Flights of fancy, flights of stairs

An infinity of little steps

Erewhon becomes Nowhere

Pass the parcel, pass the chairs, until the music decides to stop

Like the tortoise and the hare, at any spun and threaded moment

Your pace is halved yet once again

Constantly updating ancient prayers

Grow up now, step up to cope with daily cares

Life goes on and on and on, till we all become anon

Flickering shadows on Plato's imagined wall

Was clarity before the Fall?

Is there existence on the other side?

Or just a mirror image on reflection:

Eternal absence of direction?

Everything is almost nothing

From leaden roof to turkey stuffing

From concrete elephant to blueberry muffin

Solid as a rock is portentous poppycock

We are all a waste of space, I must now explain my case

We are only atoms, with nucleus one million billionth of its volume

Plus fuzzy everywhere and nowhere electron orbits

The rest is a void like Sunday morning at the Ritz

That solid chair on which you sit is mostly space

Just like most of the human race

But worry not, your body's carbon is immortal

Formed almost at the dawn of time in supernovae

When you depart this mortal coil and possibly return to soil

In about 2000 years those atoms could be anywhere

In a celeb's armpit or rock star's pubic hair

As with oxygen, maybe from invading Caesar's chest

Or Boudicca if you are blessed

106

Fingerprint file

I'm all fingers and thumbs

My prints have come - to electric memory stored somewhere

It looks over me, it looks out for me, it looks everywhere

It has my voice print, and my facial recognition

It even knows that on top is my favourite position

What an imposition! I wasn't expecting the Spanish Inquisition

Facial print and faecal print

Listen in, and listen out, listen, honey, don't go without

Your Beretta 950, stay shifty, they know what we think

They know it all, every blink, every kink

CCTV, every corner, every street, every chink

Stay with me, let's have another drink

Everything you say or do, our new Stasi keeps its eye on you

What you read, what you say, where you've been this sunny day

Like a thousand strands of summer hay

Don't think twice, it's not alright

Don't think once, just appear to be so nice

Beware the casting of the dice

The cat's around, we are the mice

Folly days and horror days

Formerly known as 'holidays'

Now just call me a bluff old stickler in the mud

But are not holidays meant to relax one's bod?

Not designed for spitting blood, a rest that is meant to de-stress

A vacation that is meant for contemplation

A stuffy airport is the last resort

Germs caught, queueing fraught, disgusting food bought

Get taken short, seating sought, tickets fought, evil thought

Tempers wrought, documents not brought, muscles taut

Kids distraught, no support, curses export, nostrils snort

The other way to ensure no relaxation is to pick a motorway

Upon a busy summer day, surely there is a better way?

Don't drive, don't fly, why comply?

You return to go through torture yet again, isn't this a bit insane?

Go by train?

Except can anyone explain why it's cheaper for 3 nights full board

Plus flights somewhere abroad than one single train ticket of 200 miles?

It's got me floored, I need a holiday, at home, talking to my garden gnome

I wandered lonely as a Guardian reading Tory voter

As rare as whelks in South Dakota

Or Sid Vicious in a boater

Or seeing an aesthetic looking floater

Or hearing 'Nessun Dorma' sung by a bloater

Or a gloater just put on toilet cleaning rota

I searched and searched for a sane Boris Johnson fan

Less likely than a welcoming abattoir's quiche flan

Or a Cabinet with elan and who would carry the proverbial can

Or anything ever going to a plan

Or ministers' promises not flushing down the pan

I sought enlightenment in the press

Less possible than Mike Tyson in a dress

I looked for policies to halt UK decline

Less imaginable than slugs without the slime

I hoped to spy some crime deterrent

They say a policcman was seen last month in Kent

I tried to find a Civil Service office fully manned

Less chance than bearable music in Poundland

I hoped that H and M would be discrete

Less likely than trainers without the smelly cheesy feet

I want to compose witty bon-mots

But will just as likely pick my nose

I must teach my pussy cat not to hunt and kill

As expected as Marilyn Monroe at my window sill

I strolled as lonely as a rational schitzo

Less likely than the Pope grooving in a disco

I want to have the aura of Humphrey B.

As likely as Beluga and champers served in KFC

I want to acquire a dazzling rapier wit

And not to be a miserable old git,

And get paid oodles for writing shit

As impossible as a deficit surfeit

Last working class hero (Fred Dibnah MBE, 1938 - 2004)

You climbed to fame at first, reached the top as a steeplejack, but steam engines were always your life-long passion. As a Bolton boy, the smell of coal, steam and oil, once sampled, were never forgotten.

The noises of steam engines, steam trains and steam rollers held you in sway: clanking, hissing, puffing and chuffing, bogies and track squealing The sight of gleaming brass and pistons moving was so appealing, steam engines are alive, but led to wives getting brassed off and sometimes leaving.

Years spent renovating an old Steam Roller was your obsession (as also was a pint or two). Then TV discovered you, a real working man, with the perfect working class name, with accent to boot, all capped off with that flat cloth cap. .

The public took you to their heart, 'He explains things AND he can make them too', they said. King Coal, Queen Steam, a Jack of all trades you were indeed.

Connecting rods connected, flywheels span, you were always a gentleman. A head of steam, but beyond your time, at heart you were a Victorian man. You are missed, you left too soon and now you're back at the top of that great stack in the sky.

111

Lichen

Lichen, lichen, on my wall, who is most likely to outlive us all?

You greeted me when I arrived, orange rings on Cotswold stone

In those forty years and more, you have grown an inch maybe

So few realise that you really are alive

I surmise you've lived two centuries or more

In 1820 George IV became King, Constable began the Hay Wain

But you might have missed all that, I suppose

But you have seen countless moons, so many Junes

At night the Seven Sisters and Orion look down on you

The Sun moves across its heaven and warmly beams down at you

The wind and rain refresh the stone that you call home

Insects fly and land nearby, the postman hurries past your place

Blackbirds, robins and bats all swoop aloft

Horses once, now cars go past and throw out fumes

The air has changed these last decades

But you remain, such pleasant, peaceful orange shades

That grace the wall and will be there when I am carried out

And in the next two hundred years and more

You will still be here, I'm sure, to welcome people to the door

Life coach

Movement and moment, travel to unravel

Perched in my nice comfy squishy seat

On life's highway, looking down

The coach speeds on, passing varied vistas

I relax and take in all the clouds, suspended as we race together

The roadside trees hurry by in the other direction forever

I glance at cars as they overtake and sometimes brake

No clouds for them – it's concentrate, concentrate

A large red car, young woman at the wheel, accelerates away

What are her thoughts, what has passed for her today?

What mixtures of emotions, whilst passing along eternity road?

What secrets, what intrigue, what has gone, what is to come?

I pick up my book, read a page,

The crossword suggests I'm comatose

I gaze into the clear blue sky, my spirit is content and glows

I can let the driver manage all the contra-flows

Heading to the Megalopolis

Whilst experiencing Mega-lot-of-bliss

Malice in blunderland

As a paid-up pessimist (B.Pess. Degree from Jaywick Sands University)

Who is often pissed and round the twist (You get the gist?)

And a half-glass empty-ist

It seems to me that stupidity and greed are on a spree, or is it just me?

Am I perhaps being a touch curmudgeonly?

But tell me anything that our rulers have ever got right

The MOD seem free to give us boats you wouldn't sail on Bishops Moats

(I've heard of 'Plain sailing' but 'Sailing without planes'?)

They give us tanks that can't be driven, tanks for the memory

Of countless millions down the Swanee

WMD that did not exist, an Opposition who did not insist

To look at the evidence which would have made sense

(A little knowledge is a dangerous thing)

Which ironist with a malicious twist gave us 'Smart Motorways'?

And knighthoods for getting it all wrong

Or acting like a demented King Kong. a bridge too far, a fridge to hide in

What the Butler didn't see - Trade though Dover? Bowled him over

Green Policies that an intellectual flea could not agree

Can't they think? It's enough to make one turn to drink

Money talks

Sound Money, but I can't hear the notes

Funny Money, but I don't get it, and where's the joke?

Laundered Money, is it really clean and ironed?

On the money, in the money, are good positions

Money is honey and it buys the best friends

Make a cache of your stash or take a position

Short or Long, but both can go wrong

Bitcoin is the current fad

Crypto to the crypt or you could be had

There's nothing to back it

It's a pyramid front

So don't be such a stupid ****

MP rap

One gay day, while fancy free, I decided to become an MP

I'd tasted grass and been beaten on the playing fields of Eton

Whipping was de rigueur, my gander was always cooked and eaten

Fagging and those adolescent dreams of shagging

Getting tight with lots of youthful gagging

Tuck shop always full of sticky buns

Lots of chums, always cracking witty puns

Then to All Souls to avoid the proles and to borrow Daddy's Rolls

Bullingdon was jolly japes, excess champers and summer hampers

Start to climb the greasy ladder, got a position and an easy number

Journalism for the dumb and dumber

Bent the rules, bent the truth, bosses hit the proverbial roof

Always had the gift of the gab, peasants always thought me fab

Got selected by blue rinsers and the colostomy bag owners club

Recruiting cronies from those long hours spent in local pub

Stuff the polls, ignore the trolls, sod the plebs, horizontal jog some debs

Voted in by those who would choose a monkey with a blue rosette

Proving what you see is what you get

Mr Drab 2023 outright winner

You were so naturally a Mr Drab

You have the charisma of a concrete slab

And all the aura of a syphilitic scab

You are as pointless as a COVID booster jab

As slow-witted as an Alzheimer ridden crab

And intriguing as a freshly sluiced fish monger's slab

In the Cab but little gab, and little intellectual flab

Seeking the attention you always failed to grab

Were you produced in an artificial unintelligence lab?

If you were food you'd be a polystyrene foam kebab

No-one could ever think of you as fab

So uncivil servants wielded that fatal stab?

Now will the Speaking Circuit want your blab?

Less likely, I think, than a potted cactus in rehab

North winds

Things have changed

There is a chill that sweeps across the northern shores

Unleashing dark riders from concealed recesses

A tempest Prospero conjured, avenging past excesses

Signifies a newly ordered world

The apple carts will be upset

The new broom has such cruel and savage spikes

A spring cleansing, a purge is pending

Oblivion comes to those who wait

No delay to this future, most take the bait

Three Sisters have woven all the threads of Fate

The dark riders are approaching the road of strife

The Sibyl just sits alone and muses

Damocles hangs from the silver thread

The North winds blow the status quo away

Tomorrow may not be another day

Evil has severed his magic chain

Maybe augers humanity's last refrain

Nothing works

Have you noticed nothing works as should?

The NHS, Education, Defence and Police

(Don't mention it, 'cos you might 'breach the peace')

A body politic so paralysed, so despised, deteriorates before our eyes

Greed, incompetence and corruption hold sway

How can it last another day? But last it does

It's irreversible decay

Too many people spending money they don't have

On slave labour goods coming from abroad

Junk they cannot really afford

I'm so abhorred, I feel so floored

Dear lord, please put me in a mental ward

The official marmite sandwich construction, consumption and safety manual

International Edition: NATO approval (Ref. SSM / 1X213 / 99 / 69 / X-G-REV 22.7 / 01.04.2022)

This incorporates Ethical, Racial and Gender regulations relating to Marmite Sandwiches

The following organisations have contributed and should be consulted as necessary

The Marmite Sandwich Advisory Board

UN Marmite Sandwich Council

Pentagon Marmite Sandwich Committee

The Marmite Sandwich Security Working Party (MI6)

The Secret Salt Police (Room 101)

Marmite Sandwich Hot Line (24 / 7 i.e. you will be charged £ 24 and 7p per minute)

Marmite Sandwiches in Outer Space Cape Canaveral Regulatory Organisation

Church of England Marmite Sandwich Burial Advisory Commission

The Vatican: Marmite Sandwich Prayers

The Sisters of Perpetual Indulgence: Marmite Sandwich Chapter

Chapter 1: Sandwich Construction

The construction environment must be sterilised and face masks worn. The bread slices are to consist of both brown and white bread slices to ensure racial diversity. The butter must be a least 1 mm thick and checked with a micrometer. The marmite must then be applied in a gender neutral fashion.

The top bread slice may then be applied.

Chapter 2: Sandwich Consumption

Remove mask before attempting to eat. Sterilise hands or use an official crane if hand-less. Rotate sandwich to point diagonal edge towards the mouth and open mouth. Insert portion of sandwich into mouth, close jaws, bite and MASTICATE.

Marmite sandwiches may be eaten even while changing gender, on a bender, taking surrender, being a defender, when a big spender or young pretender

Chapter 3 Safety Notes

If in doubt about eating seek medical advice or ring the Hot Line in an emergency. Eating is known to prolong life. Excess eating may lead to obesity and you being called a FAT GIT. Remember to swallow.

After eating you may feel the need to EXCRETE, this is perfectly normal and is nothing to be ashamed of unless you do particularly whiffy doo-doos. If in doubt consult the POTTY TRAINING INSTITUTE, 10 Downing St. SW1

Only here for the bier

I was a teenage existentialist

From early age, about life I always wondered

As through my early years I blundered

I read some Kant then took a Schopenhauer

And squeezed a spot or two, then Mum shouted: 'Come on down for tea!'

It was baked beans yet again

At my side was Wittgenstein as I applied the ketch-up

His Tractatus was as heavy as Auntie Mabel's custard

My mates came round to play football

They said don't be a Kant, but I said no, I had to master Mr Plato

Mum got cross and said 'Get out, you silly couch potato!'

Whilst pals got into heavy metal, I had heavy books

Whilst mates had dates, set light to their farts and played with their parts

I was a teenage existentialist

No abuse of the wrist, never got pissed

Philosophers I read them all, well actually in parts

No pubs for me, no booze, no darts

Descartes, a la carte, took to heart: 'I am'

Looked on my plate - Oh no! Not again, bloody spam!

I was a strange creature - could even spell Nietzsche

With family off to Butlins

So I took light reading, Spinoza, Heidegger, Rousseau and Mill

Surely they would give me a thrill, so I would know what life's about?

But met a girl, fell in love, and now she's up the spout

If you need these books, just give me a shout

So why are we here? Truly only for the bier

Premonition: cataclysm

I listen to the swirling stream

Unclear portents, what might they mean?

I sense it in the autumn breeze

I hear it in the curlew's cry

I see it in the raven's eye

I glimpse it in the changing sky

I feel it in the oak grove's sway

I taste it in the morning dew

Something final comes this way

Restless spirits in the hedgerow green

A presence no mortal has ever seen

A comet races across night sky

I spy it high over sarsen stones

Touch stone to glimpse the future and the past

The path is now decreed, it seems

A future calculated on this day

Please take away this power to foresee

Neither sage nor seer I wish to be

I pay a visit to the Holy Well

Where instead of hope and water spring eternal

Was hit by sense of gloom, of future doom

All things must pass: 'The centre cannot hold'

Determinism, no free will, therefore all must now unfold

Is the Minotaur escaping, is the Kraken now awakening?

Is Fenrir breaking his chains, will the Trumpets sound the last?

Burst the Seventh Seal, the final task?

My train of thought is fading down the vanishing track

Signals say there is no way back

No return ticket, stumped but no wicket, bales without bail

Scrambled thoughts entombed like Jonah in the whale

Dread is rising, Hell Hound on my trail, delusions still prevail

Like the Round Table without the Knights

Like the Garden without the Delights

Like a car without the engine

Like the wronged without the vengeance

Like a rose without bouquet,

Like a K.O. without the referee's O.K.

Incomplete, not making sense, a beginning demands an end

An end must lead to another start, I must ask the Sibyl to impart

The way to lead the spirit from this foreboding dark

The riddle of the glans

What lies above us, lies below us, lies all around us but no-one wants?

A specialist in dirty deeds, a naughty member, dissembler and knee-trembler?

Why it's HIM of course

They say blondes have more fun

True, of course, but at our expense and with no remorse

Pinocchio must now feel jealous

His rival's nose must nearly stretch across the Downs

He is the lie of the land, multiple excuses always at hand

Bring on the clown, give us all too many frowns

Bunter's Head, by name of Quelch, once said ' I fear you are a greedy and dishonest boy '

It's doughnuts to the left of him, doughnuts to the right of him

His tuck shop never closes, for him a bed of roses

He is the Joker, the Diddler, the Penguin all rolled into one

Then add Bogart's Fat Man and a sticky currant bun

You've got the picture, as we constantly see, wandering the land

With hard helmet, Hi-Vis jacket and a thumb stuck out

Does anyone have any doubt

Internationally lacking clout

Always putting it about

Will the truth will out?

A bridge too far, a fridge too near

Always surrounded by a shower

Not a smarty, likes to party

I must stop now to prevent my aneurism

Or a stretch in HM prison

What was wrong with Thatcherism?

Sarajevo 1914 heritage

A small squeeze for a man

But a giant step backward for mankind

Gavrilo Princip had just triggered a specific future

Now never to be born, the unknown millions

Now certain to be culled, a generation of doomed youth

Now four players were cast into their fateful parts

At that very moment of that very time

Lenin changed a key speech word

Stalin plugged makhorka into pipe of briar

Hitler sipped late morning tea, with little finger cocked

Churchill received an Admiralty wire

Did none of these feel just a merest bat's frisson?

Did none feel any premonition?

Did none feel something in their bones?

Notoriety and fame would now embrace them

Threads of fate were being spun

Repercussions still felt today

History repeats, lessons learnt or not, too complex is the
convoluted plot

An Archduke and his wife lay dying

Four weeks later, World War began

Four years later battles truly were all lost and ended

Memorial Crosses stood in every town

Red Revolution spilled red blood, devoured its children

The Four became the Three

The 1929 Crash propelled one to the fore

Belsen and Auschwitz thought up at Berchtesgaden

History heralded World War again

After 50 million slain, Pyrrhic victory was declared

East and West then acted out the Cold War

But the Soviet empire created by World War II

Fell apart, the forces of history acting through

So that single action in June 1914 is still felt

Fighting over neighbouring borders, It has started yet again

A Deity who watches such ordained events then might proclaim

'A hunter killer tribal ape with split brain

The evil that will constantly remain

So almost everything is expected and explained'

Sat in my garden

My sacred plot, my demi-paradise, my little Eden

My pots and plot of Heaven

I gazed into the yellow and the blue

The flowers gazed back and suspended all the hours

Perfect peace and perfect silence

Noiseless and eternal, away from the infernal

I fell into trance and travelled back in time

Who sat here a hundred years ago and wondered as I did

I travelled a hundred years from hence, and pondered just the same

My spirit blazed, had Gaia seized my soul?

Time past, time present and time future seemed to connect
somehow

I asked the flowers, they answered not

I asked the earth, it said there was no answer

You are mortal, you have time it said

I just exist for eternity - so just live and be content

Sentenced to life

My creators sentenced me to Life, executed by Darwinian strife

Out of darkness I came, into first new light

I howled in vain, please put me back again

I came into that world where the Apple had long been eaten

Where Lucifer had long since fallen

Where Pandora's Box had long been opened

My countdown had begun

The menu states Seven Sins, Seven Virtues and Free Will for my plate

Around my table sit Luck, Chance and Fate

All of us are served by Messrs Good and Evil

The Four Horseman have arrived but late

The Holy Ghost is there as the invisible host

It is a moveable feast but only forward, no going back

T he establishment obeys the 2nd Law which cannot be denied

Time only runs one way, tomorrow is always another day

So play up!, play up! and the play the game!

Some advice, you cannot cross the same river twice

Divide, rule and multiply, your tidy sum may be bigger than the parts

As a pawn you must reach the eighth and avoid the Knave of Hearts

Words explained in yet more words, so how can meaning ever begin?

Things are not what they seem, the Cheshire Cat morphs to a grin

Things exist, then they don't, like a dream that vanishes before the dawn

Childhood teas on summer lawns, memories now long gone

Meet the Piper at the Gates of Dawn, gather ye rosebuds and greenfly while ye may, make more than hay to keep Black Dog & demons well at bay

Time and Tide wait for no man, we are told

Mystic experiences can't be expressed, like molten silver, burnished gold

What gains a man to lose his soul?

On this Earth, Fate may curse you into a mortal First Circle

Steal the Ring to escape, but of its power you must be careful

Circular logic negates commencement, I think therefore I am, or I am therefore I think?

This circle cannot be squared, but what goes around, comes around

Everything, it seems, so run that race around the straight and narrow

Ignore the shallow, all that glitters, avoid the shadows that grow darker

Reconcile all contradictions, approach the final gate

All you can hope is to leave this Earth in better state

All else is vanity, vanity of vanities

The cemetery clock's hands turn out to wave to you 'Goodbye'

The clouds above, I'm sure I heard one heave a sigh

Return to eternal dark and earth, or possibly the soul rebirth

Shine a light

In the gloaming

Before the day is done

And I have frittered yet another one

Walls forlorn, indifferent pavements

Towering blocks that bend to hem me in

Intoxication is wearing off much faster

Current numbness, long forgotten laughter

Lights shine above from cosy dwellings

Please let that light shine down on me, too

Lighten my darkness, give me a better tune

Let the good Lord shine his light on me

Or I will need to score quite soon

Returning to a squalid squat

To accept life's fate, is this my lot?

There will always be a fix

The darkest hours are before and after the dawn

May the good Lord shine his light on me

I push the needle in and then float free

Sixth experience

The clocks chime denoting the passing of the hour

Flames in the fire flicker, unable to express the moment

Touch is slumped deep in the sofa, deep warmth on flesh

Taste is crisp green and the juice of the meat, the fruit of the vine

Aural is choral, a magnificat or perhaps something in D Minor

Aroma is coal, wood and cigar smoke

Alcohol and nicotine have worked their spell

Dendrites and synapses spark by the million in my skull

A near perfect merge of five senses

A sixth is also present

Cannot be identified

Cannot be expressed

Cannot be explained

Only experienced, only felt

State of failure, state of decay

Although they say that 'Tomorrow is another day'

Truly, things get worse in almost every way

State your opinion, state your case

These hit that wall, doomed to fail, doomed to fall

Like a mangy poodle's poo-poo, hurriedly removed from view

You do not matter, not at all, you are simply Mr Small

Or Mrs Small: 'an interfering twit', derided as a Mrs Mona Git

Moans and groans fall on deaf ears, seen by

The sightless, gobbed to the gutless, wondered by the witless,

Chinned to the chin-less, lashed out at the leg-less,

Spun to the spineless and mouthed to the mindless

Perhaps new balls and spine to offset inevitable decline?

Hope for the future, gaze into that crystal ball

Cross a palm with silver, pass the parcel, pass the buck

The official answer is still stuck, fancy that, it's just 'Go suck!'

So sweating in the crease of life, watch for googlies to the goolies

Say a prayer to Lady Luck and don't be out for a duck

To ensure you can escape the all pervading failing State

And take control of personal fate

Stations of the cross

Actually stations of the VERY cross

Platforms for all of us

We've paid through the nose for tickets to hell

But constant, constant announcements as well

Sound advice, much too suffice

Spewing verbal diarrhoea about

'Mind the platform edge, it's a different surface'

'The next train'.... is late

'Signal failure'....yet again

'If you see something odd'....

'Stand back'....

Actually, I'd considered laying on the track

Or using the train wheels to cut my toenails

Sunday night at a station, a one hour connection

Only me on the platform but every two minutes they inform

I'm not a dunce, just tell me ONCE

I ended up screaming at that speaker near the ceiling

Strawberry astro turf forever

Let me make you down

With a trip to Astro-Town

Nothing is natural, nature is out

So blow a raspberry at the artificial green

A fake carpet that should never, ever be seen

Cover your garden with lovely gravel

It will keep the bees away, worms at bay

As barren as a eunuch's lay

PS Last year, I think I saw a moth one day

Insects seem to drive the lumpenproletariat bananas

They can drop into your pina coladas

They might end up in your pyjamas

So banish them from all your gardens

Wildlife just isn't apple pie

And who really needs a butterfly?

Or the beetles?

Better to just let it die

Strawberry vanished fields forever lie

Sunday breakfast 1963

Tea from Empire, toast with chilled slivers of delicious butter, straight from patriotic udders, Frank Cooper's marmalade (what else?), from Oxford with a double first in good breeding and thick cut divinity, giving everlasting impunity and perpetual bad taste immunity

Look at Sunday papers with sense of dread and doubt, is Johnny Foreigner still a lout? Why do Beatles Twist and Shout, what on Earth is that about?

I hear the nearby Church bells ring out and the creaking of arthritic knees lowering in the pews, so turn back to read the news, the nation seems in quite good shape and God is still in his heaven...my goodness!.It's already past eleven!

I see the gardener pruning rambling rose and hear the hissing of the hose Just another piece of toast, I think, then down the cellar and choose the right refreshment, a '55, for the English beef which is this evening's dining

Then to consider my next speech and answer some constituents' letters, asking for assistance from their betters

Life is so demanding and cruel but Englishmen were born to rule.

The 27 blues

Poor Janis Joplin just wanted a Mercedes Benz

She tried so hard to make amends

She was dragged down by her Ball and Chain

Left this world in 1970, aged 27

Hendrix lived through Purple Haze

In the Red House over yonder

Left this world in 1970, aged 27

Brian Jones of the Rolling Stones

A King Bee when in his prime

Left this world in 1969, aged 27

Jim Morrison of the Doors

Sang 'This is the end, my friend'

Left this world in 1971, aged 27

Poor Amy Winehouse

Went Back to Black, died a hundred times before heaven

Left this world in 2011, aged 27

Robert Johnson gave us Delta Blues

Left this world in 1938, aged 27

Legend relates Johnson made a Faustian pact

Meeting Satan at the cross roads at midnight

Son House sang 'Death Letter'

Inspired perhaps by Huddy Ledbetter

Known as Ledbelly for the Blues

Lightnin' Hopkins sang about 'Fast Life Women'

Howlin' Wolf needed his sugar three times a day

Sonny Boy Williamson sang about 69

John Lee Hooker and Boom Boom

Elmore James bottle-necked at the Cross Roads

The Devil got Skip James' woman

Muddy Waters told his woman 'Please don't go'

Jimmy Reid found joy

Love in Vain

Escaping on the rail road train

For those blues remembered thrills

The blues live again

Some called it the Devil's music

For me it is both black and magic

With me it will always stay

(so you can throw away that box of Milk Tray)

The dictator's dictator (Inspired by A. Solzhenitsyn & E. Radzinsky)

The ultimate version of this breed: The deadliest tiger of them all.

Possessed of a phenomenal memory, nothing escaped his paranoia and suspicious scrutiny. Nothing could be done without his approval, those not complying would receive the customary 9 grams of lead right to the head.

His perceived enemies were now airbrushed out of existence, swept into the dustbin of history, and ground into the tundra and taiga. The cobbler's son from another place with a withered arm and pockmarked face, the trainee priest had come far and he considered his divinity and destiny.

Had he not alone destroyed the Hitlerite Fascist Hyena hordes by his cunning and liberated Europe in 1945? Did his troops not charge into battle crying 'For Stalin! For Motherland!'

Of course, the people all said they loved him but did they? The most important thing to do was never to trust anyone. He made a big mistake when he trusted Hitler and look where that had got him (not that anyone would now dare mention it, of course)

The Living God paced up and down his room. Yes, it was tough being the greatest man in the World and no point in being modest about it: one was not talking about opinions here, but FACTS.

But the immortal one felt old and tired. There was no-one of his intellect to talk to anymore since Zhdanov's death. His former cronies were now just his kittens and would all have to be culled in due course.

There remained just one final task, the war with the West and the destruction of capitalism run by international Jewry. He had a protective ring of rockets around Moscow and millions of battle-hardened troops ready at his command.

He nearly had the Hydrogen bomb (ahead of the West). The Jewish Doctor's plot would provoke the West and give him the excuse. There was just one problem, very soon to be felt, Death had slipped unnoticed into his office and was just about to lay a hand on his shoulder

The end

No more walks down country lanes

Visits to the sea by train

Cream teas near to a sunny beach

Pints of beer and clouds of tobacco smoke

Friends and family to jokingly provoke

And the natural mystic we may sense

Lifetimes' memories enmeshed in the brain

Recalling roads that I can never walk again

Vanish, then just flesh, blood and bone is lain

In the dark life giving and forgiving earth

With perhaps a brief Obit., or an enigmatic epithet

Perhaps to await the final trumpet

146

The tower

A traveller rode on a chestnut steed

Along the dusty, lonely road

A dark stranger joined him at a cross roads

And asked the traveller if he wanted company

'Pray introduce thyself, good sire', the stranger spoke

The traveller replied 'I am the prince of this fair land

So must travel incognito, as you must surely understand '

The dark stranger looked into his eyes and then replied

'You must guess my name, my friend

If you are wrong, you will be eternal company for me

If you guess right, then I will permit you to go free'

The traveller answered 'Then you must be Death, it seems to me'

They rode together silently and then the stranger said

'You seek wisdom, love and peace of mind,

You must find the hidden tower of the burning heart

Its mysteries and wisdom to you impart'

Then a raven flew closely by and caught the traveller's eye

When he looked back, the dark stranger was no longer there

But now a gold ring lay on that ground and gleamed

The traveller slipped it on to finger bare

He hurried on towards the setting sun

Imagining a dark tower besides a lake, beneath a moon

Years went by, the traveller prince returned to his castle

No tower, no love, no peace of mind

He took the ring off and threw it in the fire

Then he saw a tower surrounded by a blinding light

A female voice said 'walk into the flames,

You have nothing to fear!' the maiden now exclaimed

'You were always that tower you sought

You abandoned gold to make this gain'

The prince stepped into that burning golden light

Out of time, out of earthly mind and sight

To haven and back

I took the old track past the lake and wondered, as I sometimes did, if the right incantations when reprised would cause Excalibur to arise

Past the golden swaying grain, Elysian fields in all but name and down the hill to cross the old rail track when steam was once king and carried children to the sea with buckets, spades and much glee and for parents' slap-up teas

Entering the tangled wood I felt the coolness, a sense of calm and peace. Sturdy trunks were all around, cemented to the earth and ground. I walked awhile and found where centuries ago the imagined Witches Hovel would be

Moving even further on I came upon the secret bower that in 1955 would have concealed a Dago shower, plotting to destroy Albion's green and pleasant land, but for the vigilance of the 'Famous Five '

Emerging from the cool green canopy, out into the light, I looked up to the heavens and saw a sparrow hawk hovering so very, very high, a reminder that death is somewhere always nigh.

The Church tower stood proud against the godless age, the bell tolled for Evensong, attended by a faithful few who could each chose from far too many ornate pews

Deities had vanished from the World, in a deterministic and logical age where almost everything could be explained. No more myth or mystery and some proclaimed the end of history (just how stupid could they be?)

There just remained the evil that can never be undone

I wandered on and thought what might have passed this part of the Jurassic trail

A dinosaur perhaps, Roman soldiers, a knight in search of Holy Grail?

I reached the lonely haven by the shore and fell into a trance: that at the ending of my days, I would board a ghost ship here then sail across the shimmering sea to the Island of Departed Souls

A cool zephyr interrupted such a pleasant reverie

So goodbye sea!

Home for kippers and a lovely cup of tea

Under the influencers

Have you ever been 'Under the influence'?

Or under an influencer?

'Neath those twin implanted glories

Designed for every weather

Plus botox lips, an extra treasure

Plus a rusty piercing twixt the flaps of pleasure

Their influence and superfluence

All can be found under a Dubai sky

That's always blue without a fly

Sand is sand and the skyscrapers still scrape

You could be anywhere but you're where it's at

In-bottoms are here, in-bottoms are there

Bottoms up and bottoms stare

Bottom and Puck, do you need a tuck?

Yes, it's 'influence time', that's not a crime

She must order that skimpy bikini

That hardly covers her in-betweenies

For 100 pounds, just to be unseemly?

Mammaries R US

Thanks for the Mammary was once a bit hit

Thanks for the Mammary, can still get them in January

Don't worry about your cellulite

Everything will be alright

Yes, your body is a dreadful sight

The horses certainly will take fright

But fear not, unfair wench

Liposuction's here to stay

Your lovely fat is sucked away

A face lift is on the way: Top floor? OK

Under your Dubai sky, lots of gorillas lie

They come with tattoos, drink lots of booze

Know how to schmooze and use the loos

In Dubai say goodbye

To the News:'not many dead'

But it's 69 in your double bed

Shakespeare? Knew his sister

Milton? It's good for my drains

TSE? Got a tube, thanks, mate

Culture? I reach for my pun

Culture? It's simply not fun

Evelyn Waugh? Do you mean phwoah! ?

So piss off to Dubai

This time please, please make sure it's really goodbye

Yes, influencers are fine with me, I often ask them round to tee

Off, on my golf course in Dubai, beneath that eternal shimmering blue sky

The waist land (diet for your country)

My county town offers some delights

It also presents some dreadful sights

Don't be a chump, come view the plump

You must visit as I do

To see what junk food can do to you

Now I am fat, no doubt of that

But I was lithe in my time, in my prime

These people are so young, they must love eating dung

Schadenfreude is enjoyed, it makes me feel so thin

Tattoos and trainer shoes give me the blues

What training do they ever do?

Tattooed legs, tattooed necks, tracksuits that never see a track

Snack, snack, snack

Snack, snack, snack

People, you must lose your blubber

Or it will lead to double trouble and much bubble

'Tis sweet and fitting to diet for your country'

(Dulce et decorum est pro patria mori, modified

Wayne lowers it

He lowered his suspension and lowered his IQ

Something rather difficult from the consensus point of view

He fitted a large bore which was appropriate too

Exhausting fumes and patience from all when coming into view

It sounded all deep and throaty

But don't let him deep-throat you

Even his tyre valve caps had been personalised

A sight that one would never notice

His cam-shaft has been polished hard

But his charisma is below a tub of lard

I wish he'd big-end it all

He's got monogrammed driving gloves

When his mum wrote out the letters

And furry dice, isn't that nice?

He revs and revs around the town, there's nothing else to do

It doesn't seem to pull the birds except for pigeons' poo

Poor dipstick Wayne

Life has not been very kind to you

We band of brothers

You will outlive this day, whatever passes or God wills

You may return safely home, the rest of your life to fulfil

You may lie on the field, just covered by your shield

The scars in your mind will always linger

The scars on your body will always fade

Until the end of your time here on Earth goes

When you ascend to the Hall of Heroes

To raise a toast to all comrades, the survivors and the slain

To be forever brothers in arms

A band of brothers who are together again

We have had our time here under the sun

It is now the ending of the days, it is now the parting of the ways

Once we walked together down that path

Once we talked together, words led the way

Spiritually hand in hand, heart to heart

Not in slickness and in wealth, but in openness or wise stealth

It seems about a hundred years ago

I often pleaded with indifferent Time: Please, slow, slow, slow

The grass was always greener, the spectacles were rosier

We look together but now see completely different views

Now we hear different sounds, and we play a different game

Always drifting or just shifting through the blame

All experience is in the past, looking through the glass so dark

I now seek green pastures to lie me down in

To lie besides still waters, to restore my soul

Alone and lost, darkness falls, cold gusts chill the spirit

A dark stranger on dark horse appears, with face as yet well hidden

Time arrives. Time then freezes. Stasis is in play

Suspended fear, suspended doubt, the brief candle now goes out

The Ferryman removes the coin, a toll that all must pay

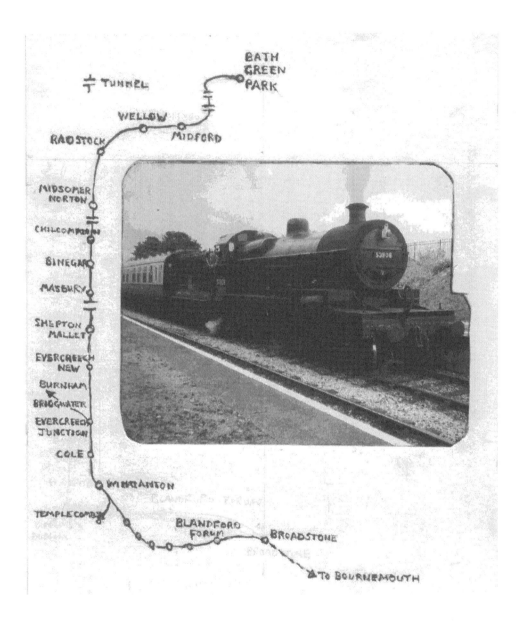

BATH
GREEN
PARK

TUNNEL

WELLOW

RADSTOCK

MIDFORD

MIDSOMER
NORTON

CHILCOMPTON

BINEGAR

MASBURY

SHEPTON
MALLET

EVERCREECH
NEW

BURNHAM

BRIDGWATER

EVERCREECH
JUNCTION

COLE

WINCANTON

TEMPLECOMBE

BLANDFORD
FORUM

BROADSTONE

TO BOURNEMOUTH

158

53808

You fired up and came alive in 1925

You steamed a million miles and more

You hauled a million tons

For nearly forty years your flame burned bright

Coal, grease, oil, and steel on steel

Smoke and steam, pistons moving

Wheels squealing, resonating down the track

Sensations now lost in time's tunnel

Along the long lamented Somerset and Dorset line

Hear an eerie whistle where ghost sleepers sleep

From Bath Green Park to Evercreech Junction

And back, on iron road, up and down the sleepy Mendips

Through Wellow, Binegar and across Cannards Grave

Moving coal, people, pigeons & boarders' trunks

Through the good times and the bad

Through war and peace, your burning heart never failed

But then one day the axe fell, and your flame went out

You awaited the welder's torch, but fate said 'Nay'

Reborn you steamed again and still steam today

Notes: Inspirations and acknowledgments

Most material referred to is available on the Internet via Wiki, You tube, Amazon and other on-line sources for no charge

My thanks to John Cooper Clarke for inspiration.

Poem titles, ideas and adapted quotes: Thanks to the Rolling Stones, The Kinks, Bob Marley, Douglas Adams, George Orwell, The Pink Floyd, T S Eliot, Baldric from the Blackadder BBC TV series, The Stranglers, Eminem, The Beatles', A E Housman and Shakespeare

Many of the poems are obviously indirect tributes to George Orwell's dystopian vision '1984'. Orwell's work has recently come out of copyright with a few exceptions which apply only in the USA.

Other dystopian novels of note are 'Brave New World' (Aldous Huxley) and 'A Clockwork Orange'(Antony Burgess)

Aspidistra vista 1936 (page 79)

A tribute to Orwell's work of the conditions of the working class prior to WWII and inspired by 'Keep the Aspidistra flying', 'The Road to Wigan Pier' and 'Down and out in Paris and London' (The latter being an account of Orwell's personal and working experiences in both cities)

The working and upper classes of the 1930s are brilliantly captured by the photographer Bill Brandt as shown in his book 'Shadow of Light'. Other artistes that recorded this environment (but in later eras) are Robert Frank's 'London/Wales' (1950s) and John Cooper Clarke's song set in the 1960s: 'Beasley Street'.

Also recommended is Martin Pugh's 'We danced all night - A social history of Britain between the Wars'

Escher feature (page 103)

'Erewhon becomes nowhere'. 'Erewhon' is a satire about Utopia written by Samuel Butler (1872) and is sometimes compared to 'Gulliver's Travels' by Jonathan Swift (1726).

'Flickering shadows on Plato's imagined wall' - A reference to Plato's allegory of the cave from his work 'Republic'.

Dalek conquest 3023 AD (page 25)

The threat by the Chief Dalek to read fellow Daleks his poetry proposal was inspired by 'Hitch Hiker's Guide to the Galaxy' by Douglas Adams. The TV Series of original radio show is well worth watching

Big mother is watching you (page 85)

In Orwell's '1984' there is a daily 'Two Minutes Hate' public ceremony when party members in Oceania are encouraged to show their hate for the enemy of the state, Emmanuel Goldstein

The hologram men (page 39)

T S Eliot's 'The Hollow Men' (1925) was the influence for this title

Comfortably dumb (page 89)

The idea came from a title of a track by the Pink Floyd actually called 'Comfortably Numb'. The live version (The Pulse concert in 1994 is one example), and featuring the guitar virtuosity of Dave Gilmour, is considered by many to be one of greatest performances of rock / pop genre of all time.

53808 (page 159)

This steam locomotive was a regular on the West Somerset private railway for many years but has since moved to the Mid-Hants (The Water Cress) steam railway.

PS. It may be having a boiler service as of 2022/3 (if you were planning a visit)

Life was fun (page 55)

An idea from Pink Floyd's 'Shine on you crazy diamond' song and their 'Dark side of the Moon' album

Shine a light (page 135)

This is a title of a track from the Rolling Stones album 'Exile on Main St.'

This song is the 'Stones-do-Gospel' track, and very well they do it too. The guitar work by their incomparable guitarist, Mick Taylor, is perfectly nuanced.

Crummy afternoon (page 22)

The quintessentially British and highly successful 1960s pop group known as 'The Kinks' released a single called 'Sunny Afternoon' in 1966 which went to Number 1 in the charts. I also recommend 'I'm not like everyone else' LIVE version (available on You Tube only, I believe)

North winds (page 118)

A real gem from the rock group 'The Stranglers' called 'North Winds blowing' gave me this title . This is from their 'Aural Sculpture' album (2001). Another classic from this group is, of course, 'Golden Brown'

Fingerprint file (page 107)

Another inspiration from the Rolling Stones: This time from the album 'It's only rock n' roll' (1974) in which Mick Jagger manages to 'out-Brown' James Brown with his vocal gymnastics. This album also contains the masterpiece 'Time waits for no-one' and their guitarist's arguably finest solo (Mick Taylor again)

Parvenu rap (page 62)

As a great admirer of the Rapper Eminem, this is a sort of humble tribute

Strawberry astro turf forever (page 139)

From 'Strawberry Fields Forever' – one of the Beatles' psychedelic influenced / influencing tracks. It was the B side to a single released in 1967 . The A side was 'Penny Lane'. BAN ASTROTURF NOW!

The end (page 145)

'And the natural mystic we may sense' (modified from Bob Marley,'Natural Mystic' 1977)

'Recalling roads that I can never walk again' (taken from 'A Shropshire Lad, A E Housman 1896)

'And perhaps to await the final trumpet', modified from Bob Marley 's 'Natural Mystic' and the last chapter of the Old Testament : The Book of Revelation

'In my beginning is my end, in my end is my beginning'

Артусов, квартира 2, особняки навозного холма, Москва, 2023г.

Printed in Great Britain
by Amazon

30052998R00093